Why Do Dogs Do That?

Real Answers to the Curious Things Canines Do

By Kim Campbell Thornton

BOWTIE
P R E S S®
IRVINE, CALIFORNIA

June Kikuchi, Editorial Director
Roger Sipe, Special Projects Editor
Karen Julian, Publishing Coordinator
Elizabeth Spurbeck, Assistant Editor
Jerome Callens, Art Director
Jessica Jaensch, Production Supervisor
Tracy Burns, Production Coordinator

Library of Congress Catalog Card Number: 96-80216
ISBN: 1-889540-01-3

BowTie Press®
A Division of BowTie, Inc.
3 Burroughs, Irvine, California 92618

Printed and bound in China.
15 14 13 12 11 10 09   3 4 5 6 7 8 9 10

Why Do Dogs ...

The Basics of Barking

Dogs bark because they have something to say. Barking may sound just like noise to us, but to dogs, barks actually say a lot of things:

"That guy in the blue uniform is attacking our front door again!"

"A strange car has pulled into the driveway!"

"Help! I've stuck my head through a hole in the fence, and I can't get out."

"Hey! You've been home for five minutes, and you haven't said hello to me yet."

Dogs communicate with us in many ways, and barking is one way they can get their point across. A dog's bark can warn us of danger or when they need help.

Dogs bark when they get excited and sometimes just for the fun of it. When you yell at them to stop, they get even more excited. "Cool! My owner's barking back at me. Now we can have a real conversation." To a dog, any kind of attention — even yelling — is something to celebrate. ●

FIDO FACTOID Dogs have been barking for a long time. More than 10,000 years ago, wild dogs hung around people's caves, scrounging for leftovers and trying to sneak in when it rained (sound familiar?). These traits were passed on to generations until eventually some dogs lost their wild side, a process called domestication. One of the results of domestication is that dogs have kept many puppy-like characteristics, including barking. For example, adult wild dogs, such as wolves, coyotes and foxes, bark very little, but their puppies bark a lot.

Car Wars

All day long, your dog tears off after the motorized monsters, barking and snapping at the tires. As each vehicle pulls away, he happily turns back with a satisfied expression. Score: Dog 5, Cars 0. Car chasing is generally a territorial reaction, often aimed at cars or trucks that drive by regularly, such as postal trucks or delivery vans.

Car chasing can also be a form of predatory behavior, usually triggered by noise and motion. Frustrated herding dogs frequently engage in predatory car chasing. After all, the herding instinct is nothing but a redirected form of the prey drive, in which the dog circles and drives his prey but does not follow through with the kill. Such an ingrained behavior can be difficult to change, but it's not impossible. ●

BEHAVIORAL BYTE As with most training, patience and consistency are key. If your dog chases particular vehicles (the neighbor's or mail carrier's), try a couple of methods.

If your dog doesn't know the drivers, ask them to stop by for an introduction. If your dog gets to know them, especially if they give her a treat, she will be less likely to view them — and their vehicles — as trespassers.

Another way to curtail car chasing is to regularly exercise your dog away from her territory. Go for long walks or hikes, play a fast and furious game of Frisbee in the park or go jogging on the beach.

These are the friendly methods. Should they fail, you may need to take more drastic and time-consuming steps, like working with a personal trainer.

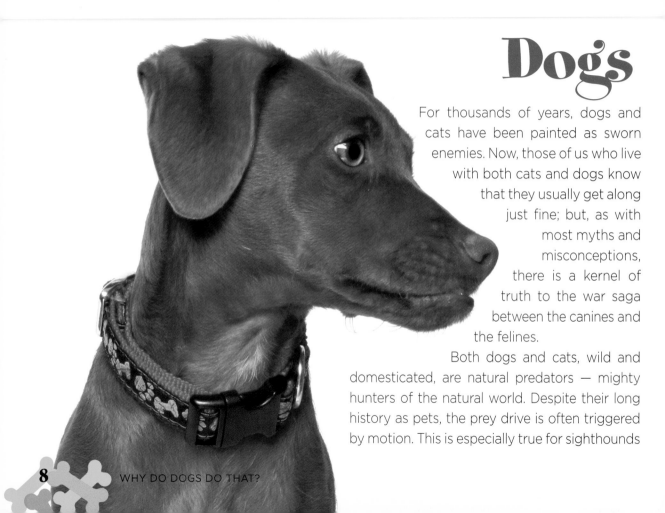

Dogs

For thousands of years, dogs and cats have been painted as sworn enemies. Now, those of us who live with both cats and dogs know that they usually get along just fine; but, as with most myths and misconceptions, there is a kernel of truth to the war saga between the canines and the felines.

Both dogs and cats, wild and domesticated, are natural predators — mighty hunters of the natural world. Despite their long history as pets, the prey drive is often triggered by motion. This is especially true for sighthounds

vs. Cats

such as Greyhounds or Salukis; terriers bred to hunt small animals such as rats and moles; and sporting breeds, all of whom were bred for the hunt.

Even though dogs of these breeds may live in a city or suburb and never hunt, instinct kicks in when a cat (or squirrel or rabbit) flashes past. The quick movement attracts the dog's attention, inciting him to chase. For some dogs, the fun is in the chase. In others, however, the prey drive is so powerful that the dog carries it through to its logical conclusion: the death of the animal being chased, if caught. This is common in breeds that have a strong hunting instinct but no outlet for their innate behaviors.

BEHAVIORAL BYTE If your dog loves to chase cats, there are some things you can try to put the brakes on her bad habit. Keep the dog on leash, even in the house if necessary, until the situation is under control. When your dog tries to go after a cat, redirect her attention to a favorite ball or toy. Playtime with the special toy should be limited to when cats are around.

Sometimes the substitution of a toy isn't enough. If your dog continues to try to chase cats, give her a leash correction or use an unpleasant sound to break her concentration. When her attention is focused on you instead of the cat, reward her. Your dog must learn that running after cats equals trouble; ignoring them brings good things. Never let your dog stare intently at a cat either; again, correct her by saying no or by using unpleasant noise.

Sometimes, dogs seem to differentiate between cats in the house (off limits) and cats outside (fair game). How the cat reacts is important, too. A cat who stands his ground and hisses or swipes at the dog is far more likely to escape than one who runs. Faced with a spitting, scratching cat, a smart dog will often turn tail.

We all know from experience that it's difficult to change a habit — especially a bad one. Changing the instinctive habit of a dog is equally difficult but can sometimes be done. Patience, consistency and sometimes the help of a trainer or behaviorist are necessary. ●

Chew on This

A dog is truly curious at heart, the Sherlock Holmes of the animal kingdom. His nose, ears and eyes provide him with a large amount of information. But to physically examine an object, a dog must use his mouth. After all, lacking opposable thumbs, his paws aren't much use at picking things up.

Chewing begins in puppyhood during the teething stage, which can last as long as a year. It helps relieve aching gums and builds strong jaw muscles and ligaments. Chewing is a natural canine behavior, but the problem with puppies is that they don't know what is OK to chew and what isn't. Think about it. If you were a dog, wouldn't you be attracted to the soft leather moccasins infused not only with the scents of the grocery store and the Grand Canyon but also with *Eau de* Human?

BEHAVIORAL BYTE Prevention is always better than punishment. If your dog is a chronic chewer, put chewable items out of reach or confine her when you can't be around to supervise her. Coat chewable surfaces with a distasteful substance such as pepper sauce or Bitter Apple. If you find your dog chewing on something inappropriate, distract her with a squirt of water or shake a can of pennies, then redirect her attention to an appropriate chew toy. Most importantly, try to catch your dog in the act of chewing on the right thing and reward her with a treat or praise.

Start your puppy off on the proper sensory exploration track, provide him with appropriate chew toys and keep your shoes on your feet or put away. Encourage him to examine his toys by making them smell and taste enticing.

Smear hard rubber toys with bacon grease or chicken fat. Hollow rubber toys can be filled with peanut butter, soft cheese or small treats. Your dog will spend hours trying to get the goods. Durable nylon, bone-shaped chews are also acceptable, but avoid real bones because they can splinter easily, causing cuts and blockages. For soft, stuffed toys, use a scent your dog loves: you! Place the toy in your dirty clothes hamper for a few days so that it develops your familiar scent. But don't make the mistake of letting the dog chew your old, worn-out shoes or clothes. He doesn't know the difference between holey sneakers and brand-new Nikes.

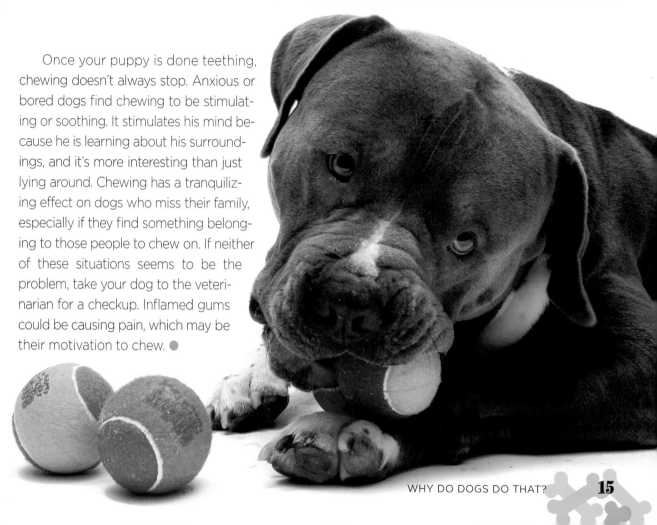

Once your puppy is done teething, chewing doesn't always stop. Anxious or bored dogs find chewing to be stimulating or soothing. It stimulates his mind because he is learning about his surroundings, and it's more interesting than just lying around. Chewing has a tranquilizing effect on dogs who miss their family, especially if they find something belonging to those people to chew on. If neither of these situations seems to be the problem, take your dog to the veterinarian for a checkup. Inflamed gums could be causing pain, which may be their motivation to chew. ●

Tilt-a-Whirl Tales

Where would we be without dogs? They sit with their heads cocked, listening attentively as we pour out our woes or joys. They must understand every word we say.

Well, not necessarily. Dogs definitely hear every word we say, whether they understand them is a different matter. A dog's sense of hearing is incredible compared to our own.

At low frequencies, dog and human hearing is similar, but dogs have us beat when it comes to hearing high-frequency sounds. Sharp hearing is a must for predators, such as dogs, allowing them to hear prey animals that often communicate with high-frequency sounds.

But it's not just the dog's ability to hear that is so interesting. It's how he does it. By orienting his head in the direction of a sound and manipulating his ears, a dog can detect the source of a sound in as little as $1/600$ of a second. Canine ears act as antennae. The *pinna* — the external ear flap — is mobile, allowing each ear to be pointed in different directions or in the same direction.

Ear position is also a means of communication. When a dog's ears go forward, it's usually in response to sound or a new situation. This dog is indicating great interest; he wants to know what's going on. Because dogs are pack animals who must pay close attention to sounds and body language to get along, listening is important to them in a social context. That's why dogs listen so intently to us and why they so often seem to read our minds. Their hearing ability and observational skills allow them to interpret

certain tones of voice and even to learn how to spell. Doesn't your dog know what w-a-l-k or c-o-o-k-i-e means?

Despite their auricular talents, dogs are known to have selective hearing. So the next time you call your dog and he doesn't respond, you'll know he's either going deaf or is choosing to ignore you. To test his hearing, try whispering his name or rattling a box of treats to get his attention. ●

FIDO FACTOID Dogs can hear a wider range of frequencies than we can. While we are similar in how low we can hear sounds, dogs can hear nearly double what we can on the higher end. Dogs can hear noises up to 45 kilohertz; humans, only 23 kHz.

Can You Dig It?

Dogged digging is a basic part of the canine lifestyle. A nice, comfy hole makes a great bed; dogs around the world have known this for millennia. In the north, ancestors of Alaskan Malamutes and Siberian Huskies dug holes in the snow, where they curled up with their tails over their noses to keep warm. Today, malamutes and huskies are still known as mighty diggers, but now their living conditions have changed. Bred for cooler climes, a "California" malamute or a "Florida" husky is likely to dig to form a cool bed, especially during hot summers.

Other reasons dogs dig are for protection, storage, prey and entertainment. Wild dogs dig dens to protect their young from storms and predators. Canines use holes as pantries or refrigerators. They catch and eat a big meal, dig a hole and bury the leftovers for later. Of course, the next time they're hungry, they have to dig out their doggie bag.

Some breeds, notably terriers, were bred to dig. That's how they find their prey: tough tunnel- or den-dwelling creatures such as badgers, moles and foxes. These types of terriers with short, strong legs, like Cairn Terriers, Rat Terriers, Scottish Terriers and Skye Terriers, are built for digging.

Just like humans, some dogs dig for the shear entertainment of the dirty act. The scent of turned earth is fresh and exciting to a dog, whose nose is more highly developed than our own. What could be down there? The possibilities are endless! And, digging is fun, especially when the dirt goes flying.

The brighter and more bored your dog is, the more likely he is to dig. After all, excavation and construction are time-consuming activities. (Dogs would probably make pretty good pale-ontologists.) Digging gives a dog left alone in a backyard something to do to pass the time. ●

BEHAVIORAL BYTE If your dog has gone from being a Bull Terrier to a bulldozer, there are several things you can try to solve problem digging. If it's too hot outside, relocate your dog to a cooler area — a shaded part of the yard or inside the house. When you catch her in the act of digging, firmly say "No!" and then distract her with a toy or game.

Houdini dogs, those who dig to escape, require a little more effort. You may need to place a concrete or wire barrier beneath the fence to keep them confined. With a hardcore hole-digger, who digs purely for the fun of it, you may have to compromise a little. Try setting aside an area of the yard where it's OK for your dog to dig. Spike the area with treats and toys to make it attractive.

The only foolproof way to prevent digging is to supervise your dog whenever she is in the yard. Attention is the best antidote to boredom.

Yummmm, Grass

Grass is the last thing we would expect a member of the order *Carnivora* to eat, yet eating grass is a common dog behavior. They nibble delicately, grazing the yard as if they were cows. Then they go inside and throw up on the antique rug passed down in your family for generations.

It's often a matter of great concern to dog owners when their pets eat grass. They take their dogs to the veterinarian, write to dog magazines for advice and ask all their friends what they think is the matter. The fact is, eating grass is a pretty harmless activity. As far as we can tell, dogs do it just because they like it.

Eating grass may also fulfill an instinctual need for greenery in your dog's diet. Wild dogs eat every part of their usually herbivorous prey, including the grassy contents of their stomachs. It could be that grass provides fiber or certain vitamins and minerals that are not typically found in kibble. Not all dogs throw up after eating grass; and some dogs seem to enjoy it as a regular part of their diet. If your dog enjoys eating grass, you might consider growing a small planter of grass just for him because outdoor grass may be treated with pesticides or infested with parasite eggs. ●

FIDO FACTOID When your dog wants a snack, try a few pieces of plain popped popcorn. Make sure there is no butter or salt on it, though. She doesn't need any extra flavoring. Other low-calorie snack ideas included small pieces of vegetables, like broccoli and carrots.

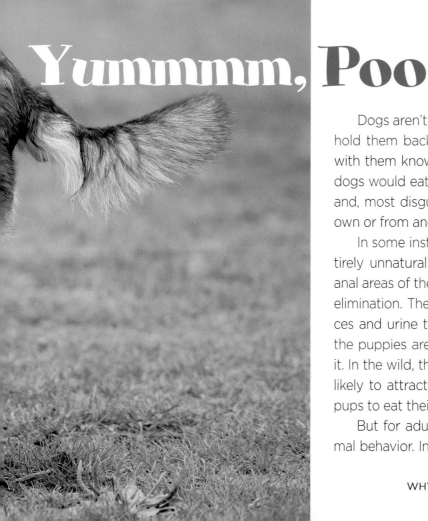

Yummmm, Poo

Dogs aren't finicky. None of our social mores hold them back, no way! Those of us who live with them know that given half a chance, most dogs would eat anything: vomit, rotting roadkill, and, most disgusting of all, feces — either their own or from another animal.

In some instances, eating poop is not an entirely unnatural behavior. Mother dogs lick the anal areas of their newborn puppies to stimulate elimination. Then, they swallow the resulting feces and urine to keep the nest area clean until the puppies are old enough to learn not to soil it. In the wild, this habit also makes the area less likely to attract predators. Nor is it unusual for pups to eat their mother's feces for nutrients.

But for adult dogs, eating poop is not normal behavior. In many cases, it is believed to be caused by the most common of culprits: boredom. Dogs who lack interesting toys, regular human companionship, or a change in scenery or activity may turn to poop eating for want of anything else to do. They may eat their own feces or the feces of other animals. Some dogs especially like snacking out of the cat's litter box. Maybe it's like a Tootsie Roll candy to them.

As unappetizing as it may seem, eating poop is not necessarily a harmful practice, although in some cases it can cause parasite infestation. And,

of course, face licking is out of the question!

There is only one surefire way to stop your dog from eating poop: prevention. Walk your dog on a leash so you can pick up after him immediately. Put the cat's litter box in an area that is inaccessible to your dog. Muzzle him when you can't supervise him in the yard. Other options include teaching your dog a Don't Touch cue or adding pancreatic enzymes (found in some commercial products) to his food to make the feces taste bad. ●

BEHAVIORAL BYTE If your dog has developed this practice, try livening up her routine. Regular exercise and toy rotation may add some interest to her life. Feeding more than one meal a day is another way to relieve boredom. It's always a good idea to schedule a veterinary exam for a dog who eats feces. A parasite infestation may cause a ravenous appetite, leading her to eat anything she can find. Or, your dog may have a nutritional deficiency.

Discuss your dog's diet with your veterinarian, and ask about providing the dog with vitamin B supplements. Sometimes a change in diet — to a food that is higher in fiber, fat or protein — will solve the problem.

WHY DO DOGS DO THAT?

The Facts

Behind Fetching

The first job dogs did for humans was to hunt. But it wasn't until the mid-19th century that modern hunters took the dog one step further and taught him to find fallen game and bring it back, undamaged. That's what retrievers, such as the Labrador or Golden, were trained to do. Retrievers are specialists who can work on land or in water. Pointers, setters and spaniels point or flush game, and can also learn to retrieve.

Like so many behaviors, why the retriever retrieves can be traced to his wild forebears.

Wolves carry food back to the den for other pack members, especially puppies, so they can share in the feast. Retrieving ability is not limited to game, however. No one who has seen a Golden Retriever endlessly fetch a Frisbee can doubt the dog's heritage. Today the retriever's desire to find and bring things back along with his "soft mouth" — Goldens are able to carry items in their mouths without making a single scratch or dent — make him indispensable as a service dog for people who are confined to wheelchairs. ●

FIDO FACTOID There are a few ideas about where Frisbees came from, but the consensus indicates they were inspired by the Frisbie Baking Company's pie tins. College students were known to throw these tins for entertainment, and so the revolution began. Walter Frederick Morrison is credited with inventing the first plastic Frisbee, which was eventually produced by the toy company Wham-O, and even studied by the U.S. Navy.

Going Postal

It's not just the mail carrier's uniform. Don't get the idea that dogs are rebels, growling at all forms of authority. Rather, the fact that your dog growls and barks ferociously at the mail carrier is due to the way your dog's brain is hardwired.

A dog's brain programs him to stake out and defend a territory. A typical canine territory contains a den-like area and its surroundings where the dog can hunt — in other words, your home and yard. Any "invasion" of this territory sets off alarm bells in your dog's head. "Gotta protect the home turf. Gotta keep the rest of the pack safe."

In the case of the mail carrier, this scenario is played out daily.

The mail carrier enters the yard and heads for the mailbox, the dog barks and growls, the mail carrier deposits the mail and leaves. Score: Dog 1, Mail Carrier 0. That's how the dog sees it, anyway. In his mind, he has successfully driven off an intruder. ●

BEHAVIORAL BYTE To put a stop to this behavior, introduce your dog to the mail carrier so they can get to know each other and become friends. Put your dog on a leash. When the mail carrier arrives, take your dog out to meet him or her. Be happy when you make the introduction. If your dog sees that you don't view the mail carrier as a threat, she will learn that she doesn't have to protect home and hearth against this "invader." Give the mail carrier a treat to give your dog. That should seal the friendship.

WHY DO DOGS DO THAT?

Howl Goes It?

All canids (foxes, jackals, coyotes, wolves, dogs) — wild and domesticated — howl, and howls can have many meanings. Wolves have group howls before hunts, presumably to "psych themselves up" for the chase. A howl can communicate alarm or happiness. It says, "Honey, I'm home" or "Turn around and go back the way you came, stranger; this is my territory." Wolf packs howl to locate missing members, encourage stragglers on the trail, celebrate a successful hunt or the return of a pack member, or, in the case of loners, to find companionship. Each wolf has a distinctive voice identifiable by other wolves.

Pet dogs howl for many of the same reasons. Dogs who are frequently left alone may howl a summons to their human pack: "Where are you? When are you coming back?"

Often, howling is a response to other howls. Dogs who howl at the sound of ambulance sirens may be responding to the siren's "howl."

FIDO FACTOID The baying, or singing, of hounds — sometimes described as mountain music — allows hunters or handlers to locate their dogs. The comparison of howls to music is universal. As early as 1615, people used to combine hounds in a pack just to produce a symphony of sound. Many people report that their dogs howl along to the sounds of music.

Beagles, bloodhounds, coonhounds and other scenthounds howl to indicate that they have located their quarry, whether it's a raccoon, a lost child or an escaped convict.

The dogs most likely to howl are hounds and northern breeds. Some people say their dogs howl when they are happy or sad or when the weather changes. Females in heat give come-hither howls.

So the next time your dog howls, you know that he's communicating something important. With practice, maybe you can learn to understand what he's saying. ●

WHY DO DOGS DO THAT?

Get Your Paws Off Me!

"Sparky, I'm so happy to see you! What a good dog you are! I missed you so much today! That's right; jump up here and see me!"

Sparky: "Susie, my favorite human, it's about time you got home. Just wait until I jump up and show you how much more important I am than you."

Susie would be surprised to learn that Sparky's body slam was an attempt at dominance rather than a greeting. Jumping up is one of the most misunderstood behaviors, and it is one that people encourage from puppyhood. A puppy who jumps up is pretty cute, but by the time Sparky weighs 125 pounds, his jumping isn't so cute anymore.

BEHAVIORAL BYTE To stop jumping in its tracks, it's best to begin when your dog is young and easier to control, but a dog of any age can learn to give a proper welcome. Start by always greeting your dog calmly. Come in the door, put away your things and then greet the dog in a room away from the front door. If your dog tries to jump, turn aside and ignore her. Don't yell or try to knee her. Dogs will work for any kind of attention, positive or negative, but they hate being ignored. You can replace jumping behavior by teaching your dog to sit when you arrive. Reward the sit with a treat or praise.

Jumping is common to all dogs, wild and domesticated. It begins in puppyhood as a desire for food or a sign of submission. Wolf pups jump on their mother after she returns from a hunt, licking her lips to induce her to regurgitate food for them. The lip-licking behavior is also a sign of submission: "I'm sorry I was rough when I jumped on you, Ma; please forgive me."

In adulthood, the jumping behavior evolves into an attempt at dominance. The taller a dog stands, the more status he has. If he can stand over or jump on a rival, he has the upper paw, so to speak. What you may view as a sign of greeting or affection may have a very different interpretation by your dog, especially if he is large or aggressive. In some cases, the attempt to push away such a dog can have serious consequences. ●

Leg Lifts

Sometimes you wonder if you're ever going to make it around the block. Your male dog stops every few feet to lift his leg — on trees, light poles, car tires. You name it, he'll mark it. You'd think he was leaving secret messages, and in a way, he is.

A dog's urine contains scent markers that delineate his territory, inform other dogs of his whereabouts, indicate his social standing and sexual availability, and warn intruders. Dogs hike their legs to distribute scent at the highest point possible, allowing air currents to sweep it throughout the area.

That walk around the block every evening is like one long continuous canine bulletin board. The urine marker left on an oak tree might say, "Bubba was here — male Rottweiler, unneutered, likes to eat special beef chunks, looking for a good time." On the grass beneath it is a reply: "Hi there, I'm Mimi: a female Bichon Frisé, in heat, eats only from humans' plates and too hot to trot."

Your dog, Lucky, thinks Mimi sounds pretty good — too good for Bubba — so he carefully aims a urine stream at Bubba's spot on the tree, hoping to cover it with his own message: "Lucky here — say, Mimi, wouldn't you like to get together tonight?"

You may notice that dogs in common areas, such as a dog park, don't do as much leg-lifting. That's because they are all unsure of whose territory they are on, so they make an effort not to offend. Dogs who were not socialized as pups may try to mark territories in these neutral areas.

Observers have found that dogs can urine mark up to 80 times in a 4-hour period. A dog who frequently lifts his leg is expressing his dominant personality.

Very dominant dogs may even urine mark other dogs or even people. Leg-lifting is not limited to males either. Very dominant females, especially among the terrier breeds, may also lift a leg. ●

BEHAVIORAL BYTE Leg-lifting behavior is OK on walks, but it becomes a problem when the dog starts marking territory indoors. A dog left home alone may become nervous and lift his leg on furniture or walls to warn away potential intruders.

This dog may be suffering from separation anxiety. Accustom him to being home alone and reassure him that you will always return by leaving for only a few minutes and then returning. Gradually extend the amount of time you are gone until the dog is comfortable with being home alone. The dog may also benefit from staying in a dog crate.

The Joys of Toys

Throw a toy for your puppy and watch him blast off after it. He pounces, takes the toy into his sharp little teeth and shakes it wildly, growling all the while. "Kill the toy! Kill the toy!" you say with a laugh. And that's exactly what you're seeing: the killing instinct in action. Our dogs have millions of years of programming hardwired into their brains: chase, pounce, bite, eat, repeat.

Today, of course, most dogs have a more modern method of hunting: They wait patiently in the kitchen, staring up with big, brown puppy-dog eyes, as their evening meal is plopped into a bowl. But instinct is not so easily put aside.

It has been said that a puppy's play is his work. The pouncing action, which is the consummation of the chase response, appears in puppies between 4 and 5 weeks of age. It is one of the behaviors that, through play, puppies practice to become a successful dog. Although the urge to track and kill prey is in most cases no longer necessary for canine survival, the behavior is innate. Because the dog has no prey upon which to practice, he uses the next best thing: his toys. ●

FIDO FACTOID In the wild, it is believed that young wolves and coyotes who are old enough to hunt hone their play-practiced instincts by observing the adult members of the group.

WHY DO DOGS DO THAT?

Leash Laws

They were a sight. Twice a day, two Boxers loped around the neighborhood, hauling a small woman behind them. She'd stumble by, barely able to get out a hello before being dragged onward. She finally took up jogging so she could keep up with them.

Pulling can be related to either personality or heritage. Dominant dogs often are pullers. Pulling is also a behavior that is frequently seen in sled dog breeds such as Siberian Huskies and Alaskan Malamutes. It's understandable that sled dogs would be pullers — after all, that's what they were bred for. A sled dog with the personality of a commanding leader is even more likely to always be out in front. Bernese Mountain Dogs, Newfoundlands, Saint Bernards and Great Pyrenees once used to pull carts for farmers or delivery people, so they have a strong instinct to pull, too.

FIDO FACTOID A head collar, which is fashioned much like a horse halter, is a good way to control a dog who pulls. It is natural for a dog to pull against pressure, which is why so many dogs pull on their leashes. The head collar is designed to put pressure on the back of the neck, in much the same way that a dominant dog or mother dog imposes discipline, instead of the front of the throat. A head collar will not hurt your dog and is easy to use.

There are several things you can do to keep your dog from pulling on leash. The first and easiest is to teach him while he's still a puppy not to pull. If he surges ahead, snap the leash and say no. Reward him for walking nicely beside you.

A dog who pulls because he wants to be the boss needs to learn his proper place in the family. You can help reduce or stop the pulling behavior by taking the dominant position in the household. Never let this dog walk in front of you. Always walk through doors ahead of him, and feed him only after you have eaten.

A fun way to control your dog's tendency to pull is to redirect the instinct. Teach him to pull a small cart or wagon. Then, he can help you unload the groceries or do yard work. If you live in a winter wonderland, you and your dog can take up skijoring, a sport in which your dog pulls you on skis, maybe even dog sledding. Mush! ●

Smeller's the Feller

No one really knows why dogs like to coat themselves in what we consider to be disgusting smells, but theories abound. For a dog, rolling in dead fish or other stinky substances may be akin to the human purchase of a Hawaiian shirt or a flashy red dress studded with rhinestones. Being smelly makes them stand out from the crowd, and it may even make them seem more attractive to the opposite sex. If you look at it another way, the canine appreciation of foul odors can be compared to a cheese lover's appreciation of a ripe Limburger or Liederkranz cheese — both are quite stinky.

Another possibility is that the practice may serve as camouflage. Just as soldiers paint their

faces and wear clothing designed to blend into their surroundings, dogs may "wear" certain odors to hide their scent from predators or prey.

Some people who study dogs think that smelly fur may be another way dogs communicate. It allows them to say, "This is what I found when I was out hunting."

It's safe to say that this is one of those questions to which we will never have a really good answer, except to say that it's in*stink*tive. ●

FIDO FACTOID Ever wonder why your dog's nose is wet? To help her smell. A dog's brain is dominated by the olfactory cortex, the place where smelling happens. It is close to 40 times larger than humans' and the average dog has 125 to 220 million scent receptors. A wet nose means she can determine exactly where a smell is coming from. That's how she knows when you silently brought out that chicken; she followed her nose!

Make No Butts About It

There you are, talking to that really cute guy in the park, the one with the really cool Doberman, when your dog, not content with sniffing the Doberman's butt, decides to sniff the guy's butt, too. He gooses him a good one while you turn beet-red and yank on his leash, hissing at him to "stop that right now!"

If our noses had the sensitivity of a dog's, we'd probably be sniffing butts, too. Dogs and humans have individual scents, and that unnerving nose action is the canine version of an FBI check. The scents and secretions of the anus, genitals and mouth tell a dog everything he needs to know, including whether the sniffee is male or female, its readiness for mating, its social status and what it likes to eat. Now, admit it: wouldn't it be handy to know all those things before you went out on a date with someone?

Where a dog sniffs can say a lot. Friendly animals usually sniff each other's faces, heads and necks, including inside the ears. Two dogs of equal rank will sniff each other's behinds at the same time. When a lower ranking dog encounters one that is more dominant, he waits submissively for the other dog to sniff under his tail.

Another dog doesn't have to be present for your dog to learn all about him or her. Sniffing urine and feces can also provide information. The special odors produced in a dog's urine and feces allow him to mark territory, leave warnings to trespassers and attract potential mates. ●

BEHAVIORAL BYTE If your dog is too socially aggressive with people, fight fire with fire. Instead of backing away (an action your dog might view as submissive), move toward her, making her back away, and firmly tell her no. If she's sniffing someone else, divert her by making her sit or perform an obedience command that will stop the unwanted behavior.

Window Wonders

It's a classic image: a dog with his head stuck out the car window, ears flying, tongue hanging out. Why? Until now, no one has known. But after arduous research, the top 10 reasons dogs like to stick their heads out of car windows have been discovered (see below).

Now that that's settled, the next question is: Should you let your dog stick his head out the car window? The answer: probably not. Remember what your mother always said about sticking your arm out the car window? It's going to get torn off by a passing car, right? Well, not only do

TOP 10 REASONS DOGS LIKE TO STICK THEIR HEADS OUT CAR WINDOWS

10 So they can smell what's going on around them

9 So they can check out the beautiful Shih Tzu in the Jaguar two lanes over

8 Because they like to feel the wind ruffling their fur

7 Because the view is better

6 In case they get carsick and have to throw up

5 So they can howl along with the horns and sirens

4 So the wind can blow the slobber off their mouths

3 So they can grab any food that might be flying by

2 They're hoping fresh air will clear away the smell of that Rottweiler's behind

1 Because dogs just wanna have fun

you have to worry about that happening to your dog's head, there's also the more likely possibility that flying debris could injure his eyes. But if you just can't bring yourself to deny Snoopy the pleasure of the wind blowing through his fur, try fitting him with goggles to protect those puppy-dog eyes. He'll be the coolest dog on the road. ●

FIDO FACTOID If your dog loves to ride along with you while doing errands, take that next step: travel! When on a longer trip with your dog, stick to his normal feeding and exercise schedule.

Feeding in crate may encourage a better appetite if your dog becomes too distracted to think about food. Missing a meal is not a big deal but it is important to drink enough water, especially during summer travel. You can remind your dog to drink by spritzing water into his mouth from a spray bottle. Many breeders recommend bottled rather than tap water for dogs when traveling (unfamiliar water might upset his tummy).

Wag Their Tails?

Canids, dogs and their wild cousins, live in social groups with family values that are actually much like our own. They communicate with sounds and with body language such as the tail wag. A wagging tail has a variety of meanings, depending on the position and speed of the tail. (We know that the tail wag is a means of communication because dogs wag their tails only at other dogs, people or other animals — never at inanimate objects.)

The most familiar tail wag is a broad, medium-to-fast sweeping motion. Boy, is this dog happy to see you! He is showing the proper greeting given to the pack's top dog — in this case, you — indicating happiness and submission. The faster the tail, the more excited the dog.

Tail position can also convey interest, challenge, dominance, confidence, relaxation, fright, confusion or aggression. A tail that is mostly horizontal but not stiff is usually attached to a dog that would like to find out more about you. He's interested but not yet challenged or aggressive. When the tail is fully horizontal, a challenge to either another dog or a person is in the offing. The dog who walks around with his tail up but not vertical says, "I'm top dog around here." The dog who feels confident and in control holds his tail up and over his back.

A tail that is lowered but not between the legs usually belongs to a dog that is relaxed. A frightened or submissive dog tucks his tail between his legs. This is a universal signal in dogdom: "Please don't hurt me!" A dog that slowly wags his tail may be confused; he's not sure whether he should be making friends or on the attack. Watch out for dogs with bristling tails; their aggression is showing for all to see. A tail that is held high and stiff, wagging fast, is another telltale sign of a dog that shouldn't be messed with. An excited tail wag can be combined with aggressive signals at other areas of the body, so don't expect a wagging tail to be attached to a friendly dog all the time.

Who says dogs can't talk? Anyone who has studied the way a dog's tail wags knows that the canine vocabulary is pretty extensive. You just have to learn the language. ●

FIDO FACTOID Dog tails are more than just expression makers. Some dogs, like retrievers, use their tails just like they were rudders, helping them to navigate water. The tails of these swimming dogs are thick, strong and flexible, allowing them to make aquatic turns.

Care for Some Cheese with that Whine?

We've all heard the sound. High-pitched, it comes from the throat, enhanced by the sinuses, acting as resonance chambers. Depending on the situation, a whine could well be the most annoying sound a dog makes or the most *awww*-inspiring.

Whining is perhaps one of the first sounds a young puppy makes. The pup's payoff? Warmth, food and comfort. He learns early on that a whine brings attention from Mom.

BEHAVIORAL BYTE To nip whining in the bud, teach your dog that silence is golden. Ignore whining or other annoying sounds, and reward silence.

As they age, dogs learn to use this nonthreatening noise to manipulate their people, too. Who can resist that combination of puppy-dog eyes and soft whimpering? Only the most hard-hearted of humans could refuse the whine that means, "I'm so hungry," especially when it is accompanied by that soulful glance that dogs do so well.

Some dogs whine when they're frightened. The sounds of fireworks or thunderstorms can trigger major whining attacks. When concerned owners rush to soothe their whining dogs, they reinforce the behavior, teaching the dog two things: He has cause to whine and he's going to get attention for doing it. This encourages him to whine even more. ●

The Final Howl

One common answer to most questions that begin with "Why do Dogs" is: because they are dogs. It's important that you keep that in mind when training your dog. Dogs are dogs. They like to dig, bark, chase, etc. because that's what they were bred to do!

Your job as their owner and pack leader is to teach them when it's appropriate to do those things. Nobody likes a dog who barks all the time, but if you want complete silence, maybe you should get a fish. A yard full of holes is no fun for anyone, but a responsible owner would have a special area where his dog is free to dig and teach him where that spot is.

So the next time your dog is doing something that you think is strange, think about how many things you do that drive him nuts, like pet the cat, wash food (that could still be licked!) down the drain or wear clothes that aren't for getting dirty. And keep this in mind, too: Most of what dogs do is to get your attention (that's their primary reason for living!), so play with your dog, invite him on as many family outings as possible and spend plenty of quality time with him. Do that and you'll see that the real reason he does what he does is because he loves you! ●

WHY DO DOGS DO THAT?